This book belongs to

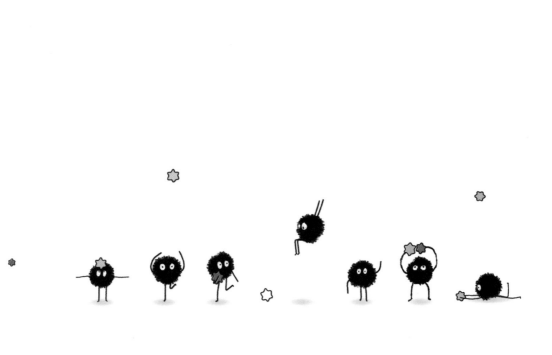

THE WORLD OF STUDIO GHIBLI

Written by

Michael Leader and Jake Cunningham

with illustrations by Lucy Zhang

WELBECK

Contents

Introduction 6

Ghibli's Heroes 8

Ghibli's Creatures 22

Glorious Ghibli Food 38

Ghibli on the Move! 52

Ghibli and Nature 66

Who's Who at Studio Ghibli 80

Ghibli's Japan 94

Around the World with Studio Ghibli 110

Index 126

Hello from Ghibliotheque!

We are Michael and Jake, and together we make a podcast called *Ghibliotheque*, all about the films of the legendary Japanese animation company, Studio Ghibli. We think that Studio Ghibli has made some of the greatest films of all time, like *My Neighbor Totoro*, *Kiki's Delivery Service*, *Princess Mononoke*, and *Spirited Away*. We love nothing more than sharing these films with other people, whether that's by watching them together on the big screen, or writing a book like the one you're holding right now.

This book is our handy, illustrated guide to the world of Studio Ghibli, a world that is like no other. Over the following pages you'll meet strong heroes, get to know wild and beguiling creatures, taste mouth-watering food, and travel via fast and fantastical modes of transportation. There is so much to explore and discover, so let's quote the motto of the Ghibli Museum in Tokyo, and say: *let's get lost, together.*

Enjoy!

Michael and Jake

GHIBLI'S HEROES

Being a Ghibli hero is never simple. Sometimes it means fighting a war to save your forest, or battling super-hungry spirits in a bathhouse; and sometimes it just means setting out into the great wide world to find your calling, with only a broomstick and trusty black cat for company. Ghibli's heroes are complex, inspiring, and fiercely independent. You've never met anyone like them.

Satsuki and Mei

My Neighbor Totoro, 1988

The two sisters Satsuki and Mei are the heroines of *My Neighbor Totoro*. After moving to the countryside to be closer to the hospital where their mom is staying, the two girls embrace all the changes the big move has on their lives.

When they first arrive at the house, they aren't scared of exploring all its dusty corners. Then, when Satsuki is at school, it's Mei that ventures into the forest, under the camphor tree next to their house, and meets their huge, huggable neighbour, Totoro.

They may be worried about their mum, and they may have to look after their dad when he falls asleep working at his desk., but they'll never have to face it alone—that's what sisters are for!

FUN FACT! ●●

In the English language version of *My Neighbor Totoro*, the voices of Satsuki and Mei are provided by two real-life sisters, Dakota and Elle Fanning!

Chihiro

Moving house is hard. Even harder is seeing your parents turn into pigs! Chihiro's adventure in *Spirited Away* is a strange and magical one. Uprooted from the life she once had, and left without friends or family, she must fend for herself in a world of odd creatures and frightful beings, but she is more than up for the task.

Once she finds herself inside the giant bathhouse, she lands a job cleaning up after the customers, and soon shows her ingenuity and bravery. She helps the Stink Spirit return to his divine form as a River God, saves Haku from his curse and solves the riddle that returns her parents to human form.

Ashitaka and San

Meet a boy and a girl on opposite sides of a destructive conflict. In *Princess Mononoke*, Ashitaka and San show us how messy and complicated the world can be, but they also offer hope for the future, too. San considers herself to be one of the wild animals that guard the forest. She hates humans for what they're doing to their home and the ancient creatures within. Ashitaka, on the other hand, has been cursed by the darkness that is poisoning the planet, and is searching for a way to find peace between all communities.

Together, San and Ashitaka are two young humans up against a stubborn world of old people and even older gods, but they show us that the right way forward is one of mutual respect and care.

Kiki

With broom in hand and Jiji by her side, the young witch Kiki, who goes out into the world and finds her independence, one delivery at a time, is one of Ghibli's greatest heroes. She might not battle bathhouse spirits like Chihiro or be a warrior-wolf like San, but the genes of those heroes can be seen in Kiki. Her adventure helps her understand her place in the world, see the importance of hard work, and learn how to triumph over any challenge that comes her way. Importantly though, Kiki doesn't always feel magical, and she sometimes feels sad too; because Studio Ghibli knows that real people, and real heroes, are just the same.

Sophie and Howl

Cursed with the appearance of old age at the beginning of the film, Sophie is a great reminder that being a hero doesn't mean being an action star. After joining up with the mysterious Howl, his friends, and his moving castle, Sophie shows that simple gestures like cleaning, listening, and caring can be the most powerful tools for supporting others.

The wizard Howl, however, is a bit more dramatic, more like a moody teenager, who can turn into a bird to help fight in the war that's destroying his land. A conflicted, occasionally tragic character, Howl is brave in battle, but also understands the importance of his closest friends, who keep him and his castle alive.

Pazu

An orphaned boy living in a mining town, Pazu is courageous and kind-hearted—not to mention a dab hand on the trumpet. When a mysterious girl literally falls from the sky into his arms, he dedicates himself to protecting her, and he journeys all the way to the fabled floating kingdom of Laputa that his aviator father once captured in a blurry photograph.

Arrietty

It isn't easy being four inches tall, but Arrietty is brave, resourceful, and adventurous. To the tiny Borrowers, even a small house is cavernous and filled with peril, especially when they embark on their daring nighttime "borrowing" missions. For Arrietty and her family, though, everything changes when a young boy, Shō, comes to stay.

Sōsuke

With his dad away at sea and his mom busy at work, Sōsuke often has much more responsibility on his shoulders than your usual five-year-old. That all changes when he finds a strange red fish on the shore, and makes a new magical friend named Ponyo, who whips up a storm of adventure.

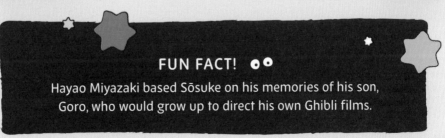

FUN FACT!
Hayao Miyazaki based Sōsuke on his memories of his son, Goro, who would grow up to direct his own Ghibli films.

Kiki's Delivery Service, 1989

How to
COSPLAY

Dressing up as a Ghibli character doesn't mean you have to be a monster or a spirit. In fact, you can cosplay as some of Ghibli's most famous human heroes quite easily.

Kiki

a red bow to tie in your hair

a loose black dress, or you could use a black trash bag

a broomstick

a black cat (or a stuffed cat if you don't own a real one!)

a red shoulder bag

red shoes

Pazu

a yellow
flat-topped cap

a white
collarless shirt

blue pants

brass trumpet

a light brown
vest

brown boots

21

GHIBLI'S CREATURES

. . . .

Studio Ghibli's films are full of extraordinary magical creatures, from greedy spirits to the world-famous Totoro. These colorful characters are memorable, meaningful, and can change how we look at the world around us.

Totoro

FUN FACT! 👀

If you look carefully there's a Totoro in every Studio Ghibli film, because after Totoro became so popular, the studio made his outline part of their logo.

What is a Totoro? The biggest Totoro has the furry markings of an owl, the whiskers of a cat, and is light enough to sit in a tree, even though they're the size of a bear! Totoro may contain parts of all these creatures, but they're totally unique. Helping sisters Satsuki and Mei experience the wonders of the woodland next to their new home, Totoro is a forest spirit—a magical, fluffy, and sleepy creature who is probably Studio Ghibli's most famous creation.

No-Face

A customer at the giant, beautiful bathhouse in *Spirited Away*, No-Face is an incredibly simple, extraordinarily memorable Ghibli creature. First seen as a mysterious, ghostly figure lurking on the outskirts of the bathhouse, after picking up an appetite No-Face balloons in size and looks more like Jabba the Hutt, eating everything in sight. But despite causing so much damage, this creature eventually becomes an ally and supports Chihiro on her next adventure, proving that even with No-Face you can still be full of surprises.

Cats

If you're a cat person, Studio Ghibli has you covered! Cats are a big deal in Japanese society and culture—they even have a special National Cat Day, every year on February 22nd.

Kiki's Delivery Service, 1989

Across Ghibli's films, you'll find a multitude of kitties of all shapes and sizes. There is the talking black cat Jiji in *Kiki's Delivery Service*, our young witch's faithful companion as she embarks on her quest to find a new hometown.

And who could forget the entire cat kingdom of *The Cat Returns*? That film is purr-fectly packed with fabulous felines, from the dashing Baron, to the frizzy-haired King.

The Cat Returns, 2002

Ponyo

Is she a fish, or is she a girl? She's both! Ponyo is one of Ghibli's most magical creations, inspired by Hans Christian Andersen's fairy tale *The Little Mermaid*, but with a magical twist courtesy of director Hayao Miyazaki.

When we first meet Ponyo, she is a little fish with ginger hair and a distinctively human face. She breaks free from her wizard father's lair, and washes up on the shore into the arms of the young boy, Sōsuke. Then, after stealing her father's magic potions, she begins to transform, first into a strange and wonderful creature with bulging eyes and chicken feet and then into a fully-formed little girl, full of curiosity and excitement to explore the human world around her.

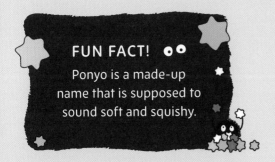

FUN FACT!

Ponyo is a made-up name that is supposed to sound soft and squishy.

Ohmu

Nausicaä of the Valley of the Wind, 1984

These giant bug-eyed beasts might seem scary, but they're just misunderstood. The Ohmu, a species that look like huge, hulking, armored woodlice, are initially seen as a threat to the people in *Nausicaä of the Valley of the Wind*. However, the Ohmu reveal themselves to be sensitive and harmonious creatures, and the real threat could be the people themselves. For even more Ohmu, read Hayao Miyazaki's *Nausicaä of the Valley of the Wind* manga, which he continued writing for ten years after the release of the film.

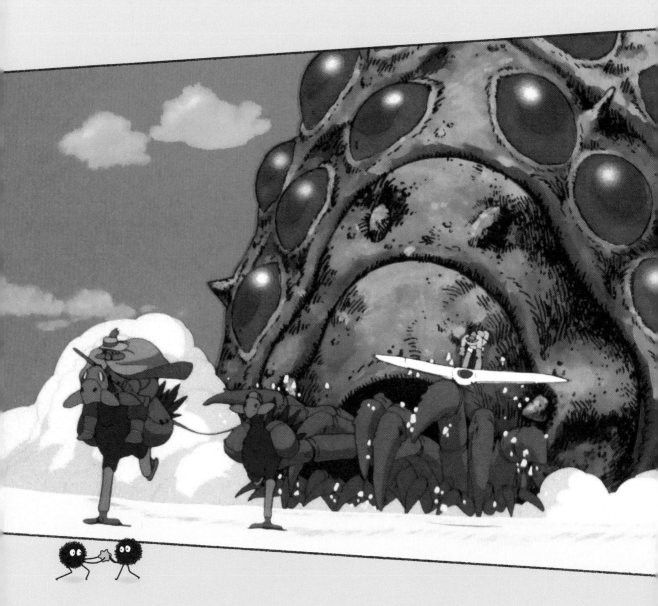

Soot Sprites

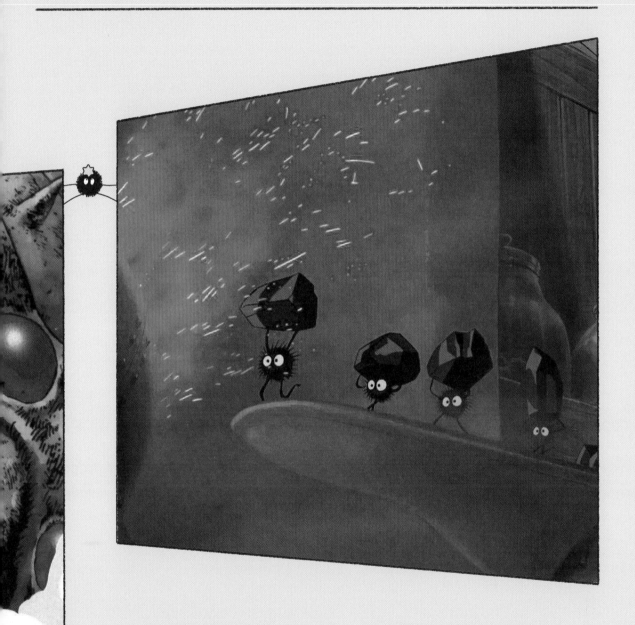

These tiny soot sprites (called *susuwatari* in Japanese) are one of the few Ghibli characters to appear in more than one film. We first see them in *My Neighbor Totoro*, when Mei and Satsuki explore the dusty rooms in their new house. They then pop up again in *Spirited Away*, in a much more obedient and magical form, carrying lumps of coal for Kamajī in the bathhouse boiler room.

The magical forest of *Princess Mononoke* is filled with these odd tree spirits, with their small bodies and round, black dots where their eyes and mouths should be.

While they don't speak, they're far from silent. The click-clacking sound they make when they nod their heads is a reminder that nature is brimming with life.

Tanuki

Tanuki, Japan's native raccoon dogs, are traditionally known to be magical, mischievous shapeshifting creatures—a perfect subject for the limitless imagination of animators.

In Isao Takahata's film *Pom Poko*, the Tanuki's forest home is being destroyed by landscapers, so they transform into warriors, ghosts, and even people to fight back; and find time to enjoy some human TV too.

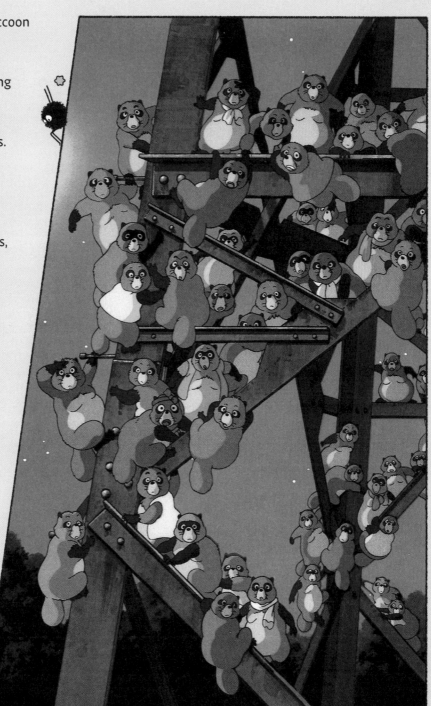

My Neighbor Totoro, 1988

How to
DRAW A TOTORO

He's a global icon and Studio Ghibli's brightest star. He is the face that graces the logo at the beginning of every Ghibli film, and the character that has been turned into everything from cuddly toys and slippers, to cream-puff pastries. It's the legend himself: Totoro. The character is known and loved the world over because his design is simple and instantly recognizable— and here's how you can draw your own.

You will need:

- A pen or pencil
- A sheet of paper

Start with Totoro's two
arrow-shaped ears.

Draw a big curved outline
for his body.

Add two circles with
dots for his eyes.

Important: Totoro's eyes are
farther apart than on a
human face!

4

Add in his nose, and catlike whiskers. Almost there!

5

Now, add his tummy. Don't forget his distinctive triangle markings!

A King Totoro has seven markings; the smaller Totoro creatures, have three.

AND...VOILA!

Say hello to your new neighbor. Try coloring in your Totoro and adding a background scene.

6

GLORIOUS GHIBLI FOOD

· ·

Food has never looked more delicious than in a Studio Ghibli film.
We dare you not to come away with your tummy rumbling.

Growing and Picking

Studio Ghibli films can make you feel happy, heartbroken, thrilled, and inspired. They can also make you very hungry! The food in Ghibli films looks so delicious! Next time you see some, you might want to pause the film just to try to take a bite.

It's not just the gobbling of amazing dishes that they care about though. They show us how ingredients are grown, like these beautiful plump tomatoes from *When Marnie Was There*, as well as how meals can be prepared, cooked, and of course eaten!

An important part of their films, meals aren't just something you quickly chomp, they're an important ritual that can teach us about the wonders of nature, the rewards of patience, and the satisfaction of a hard day's work.

Preparing

After picking their harvest, Anna and Setsu from *When Marnie Was There* take their tomatoes into the kitchen and start preparing their food. Preparing your ingredients is an important part of making any meal, everything has to be washed, peeled, and chopped correctly before you can start cooking.

Food isn't only important because of its flavour; it's about the love that goes into it too. When you put care into a dish at the start of making it, it'll taste even better by the end, especially if you have people to share it with.

Cooking

Once all the ingredients are ready, it's time to start cooking and Ghibli films show us that cooking can be a heartfelt, creative, and fun thing to do.

Take a look at the busy kitchens of the bathhouse in *Spirited Away*. These magical chefs have to be ready to fill up regular human tummies, as well as the ginormous expanding belly of No-Face. What would you like them to cook up for you?

Serving Up

From Up on Poppy Hill, 2011

When making food, presentation is everything. It is a craft all of its own. And so, scenes of characters serving up delicious meals appear throughout Studio Ghibli's films, showing both the delight in making beautiful-looking food, but also the care and attention that goes into how it is put on a plate.

Umi in *From Up on Poppy Hill* has a household full of lodgers to feed, and she takes great pride in her daily routine of putting together their meals.

Satsuki, too, takes the responsibility of making bento-box packed lunches for the family very seriously when her dad oversleeps in *My Neighbor Totoro*.

Digging In!

Once you've prepared, cooked, and served up your food, it's time to dig in and eat! Throughout Ghibli's films, they have shown us delicious, mouth-watering food and have captured the sheer enjoyment of "chowing down".

Just look at Markl, gobbling up his fried breakfast in *Howl's Moving Castle*!

Enjoy With Friends

But food can add flavor to a story, too, and that's true throughout Ghibli's films. These scenes have meaning beyond simply making your tummy rumble. Food can tell us so much—about where a person's from, what they're feeling, and what they like.

Kiki's Delivery Service, 1989

Finding some quality time between making deliveries can be hard, but Kiki and her best feline pal Jiji still take a moment to share a meal.

Pancakes, sausages, strawberries, and an all important knob of butter on top. Best served with friends.

There is one food that Ponyo loves more than any other. HAM! When Ponyo becomes friends with Sōsuke, she also falls in love with human food. One of the most magical scenes in all of Ghibli's films comes when Ponyo, Sōsuke, and his mom Lisa are stuck at home in the middle of a raging storm. The weather outside may be frightful, but inside they are safe, warm, and ready to eat. Lisa's special ramen dish, prepared and served with a flourish of "abracadabra!" is a bit of everyday cooking magic. And Ponyo's response—a wide-mouthed "wow!"—shows us that food can be truly wonderful as well as tasty!

Ponyo, 2008

Ponyo, 2008

How to

MAKE YOUR OWN RAMEN

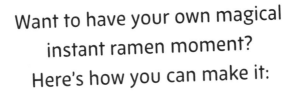

Want to have your own magical
instant ramen moment?
Here's how you can make it:

You will need:

- a packet of instant ramen
- a saucepan
- your choice of toppings
- a grown-up to help

1

Find the grown-up who's going to help you and wash your hands together! This is important to do before any cooking.

2

Decide on your toppings and start preparing them.

Ponyo and Sōsuke have slices of ham, chopped up green onions, and boiled eggs (but you can use anything). Get these ready and leave to one side.

3

2 cups

Find your packet of instant ramen, see how much water it needs, and fill up a saucepan with that amount. Get your grown-up to boil the water.

4

Open your ramen packet, put the pouches to one side, and ask your grown-up to add the noodles to the boiling water.

The packet will say how long to boil them for.

5

Once they've finished boiling, turn the heat off, get those flavour pouches, and pour them in. This will make the flavorful broth.

6

Ask your grown-up to pour the ramen and broth into bowls.

Now comes the really fun part, the toppings!

7

If you want Ponyo's ramen, place your green onions, boiled egg, and ham on top of the broth and abracadabra!

Start slurping.

But, you don't have to stop there, you could add sweetcorn, sesame seeds, spinach, bok choy, bamboo shoots, kimchi, bean sprouts, pickled ginger and lots of other ingredients. Have a look in the fridge and see what you can use to make your ramen personal!

GHIBLI ON THE MOVE!

· ·

Ever since he was a young boy, Ghibli's most famous director Hayao Miyazaki has loved drawing planes. He is obsessed. Watch Ghibli's films and that obsession is on-screen with some of the most beautiful flying sequences in film, as well as some of the most remarkable and spectacular forms of transportation ever imagined.

Flying Machines

In Ghibli films, the sky's the limit! Hayao Miyazaki's dad worked for a company that manufactured parts for planes, so since he was a kid, Hayao has been obsessed with aircraft and the tiny details behind how they work. You can probably tell that from watching his films. So many of Miyazaki's movies feature a fantastic flying machine of some sort!

These include planes that are ultra realistic, such as Porco Rosso's signature red aircraft, which is based on the Italian planes of the 1920s that are Miyazaki's favourites. Ghibli even made a whole film about engineering, *The Wind Rises*, which follows the real-life story of a young man named Jiro Horikoshi who revolutionized the design of Japanese fighter planes. In that film, we see Jiro's dedication to his craft, as he refines every tiny detail of the plane so it works perfectly.

Porco Rosso, 1992

If you're in the mood for a more magical sort of machine, there's no mode of transportation bigger or stranger than the wizard Howl's moving castle, which can change shape and size to match its master's will.

Howl's Moving Castle, 2004

Studio Ghibli director Hayao Miyazaki spent ages planning how this mysterious machine would move, designing everything down to the very last detail. The result is part house, part factory, with turrets, chimneys, and domes giving the castle something resembling a human face. This great, hulking building wanders the landscape on its spindly chicken legs, and is powered by Calcifer, a demon who must keep the fire burning or the whole thing will fall apart!

Boats

Ghibli's fascination with transportation includes vehicles made
for all types of terrain, including air, land and, of course, sea.

Ponyo, 2008

Set by the ocean, *Ponyo* is full of wonderful
waves, fabulous fish, and beautiful boats.
After arriving on land, fish-girl Ponyo finds
a toy boat, and using her magic powers

she transforms it into a full-size one,
rivalling the spectacular tankers, rowboats,
and rafts that also appear in the film.

Boats in Ghibli films aren't always about motoring toward adventure, though. In the heartfelt drama *When Marnie Was There*, a simple paddle around a lake between friends becomes a tender, emotional moment that manages to leap through the boundaries of time, without even using an engine.

When Marnie Was There, 2014

Trains

All aboard! Throughout Studio Ghibli's films, characters catch trains
to take them on extraordinary and meaningful journeys.

Such as when Anna in *When Marnie Was There*
and Taeko in *Only Yesterday* travel from the big
city for life-changing visits to the countryside.

Or, in *Spirited Away*, when Chihiro and
No-Face take the mysterious, one-track
railway out across the landscape to Swamp
Bottom to meet with the witch Zeniba.

Spirited Away, 2001

But even everyday train journeys can be magical—after all, you never know who might turn up as an unexpected fellow passenger.

When Shizuku is travelling into town in the early scenes of *Whisper of the Heart*, she is surprised to spot a cat commuting alongside her! When he hops up on the seat, looks out the window, and dutifully disembarks at his chosen stop, she can't help but follow him—just to see where the story takes her.

Whisper of the Heart, 1995

Catbus

My Neighbor Totoro, 1988

In a Studio Ghibli film, even the most mundane things become magical. If you've ever had to wait around in the rain for the school bus, you'll know how boring that can be. But what if your bus turned into a cat!

One of Hayao Miyazaki's strangest creations, the Catbus has the wide eyes, whiskers, and fur of a feline, and the familiar bench seating of a coach. A companion to Totoro, the Catbus can be found racing around the woodland of Satsuki and Mei's new forest home; and when Mei gets lost, it's the Catbus who saves the day, providing an express trip across the treetops to help reunite the sisters.

Kiki's Broom

Kiki's Delivery Service, 1989

Where would a witch be without her broomstick? Nowhere! So when Kiki sets off to find her place in the world, she takes flight on her trusty broomstick, which was given to her by her mom. Even though she's a witch, Kiki only really has one magical power: the ability to fly. That means that her broom is even more important. It's how she explores the world around her, and, when she sets up her delivery service business, it's also essential for her job.

Come rain or shine, her mom's broom helps Kiki through all her travels.
But when it is broken, the young witch must find a new broom to make her own.

The Wind Rises, 2013

How to
BUILD A PAPER GLIDER

The Wind Rises is about a plane designer named Jiro Horikoshi, a man who's totally obsessed with drawing aircrafts of all kinds and is constantly dreaming up unique, fantastical new ones—he's a lot like Hayao Miyazaki!

In one lovely scene, Jiro throws a paper plane that flies towards a woman named Nahoko, who becomes his wife. Soaring through the sky and dancing on the wind, Jiro's small paper version shows why he must be so good at designing full size planes too.

Here's how to make your own...

You will need:

- a pen or pencil
- a sheet of paper
- a ruler
- a pair of scissors
- a glue stick

1

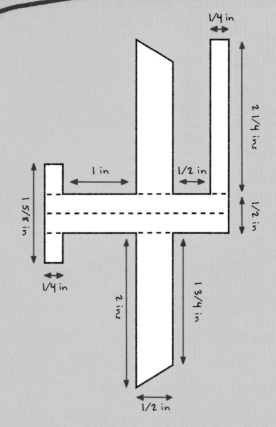

1/4 in

2 1/4 ins

1 in

1/2 in

1/2 in

1 5/8 in

1/4 in

2 ins

1 3/4 in

1/2 in

Carefully, use your ruler to draw out this design on your paper, making sure you follow the measurements.

2

Cut out the design using scissors and fold it in half.

3

Use glue to stick together the middle of the plane, but don't glue the wings, tail, or the nose.

4

Fold out the wings and roll the nose up around the end of the plane. Glue it tight!

5

Let it fly!

GHIBLI AND NATURE

Studio Ghibli's films are filled with moments of wonder that make us appreciate the world outside our window—and become aware of the delicate balance between nature and civilization.

Totoro, Satsuki, and Mei

My Neighbor Totoro, 1988

When Satsuki and Mei move to the countryside in *My Neighbor Totoro*, they are right in the thick of nature, from the rolling fields that surround their house, to the camphor tree that is right outside their door, which is home to the clan of Totoro creatures that show them a new way of looking at the world around them.

Even that most unwelcome of things, being stuck in the rain, is turned into something magical and delightful when Totoro is involved. When Satsuki and Mei are trapped in a downpour, waiting for their dad to get home from work, out comes Totoro, who is not only puzzled by the appearance of an umbrella, but is also overjoyed by the sound of rain drip-dropping on top of it.

Spirit of the Forest

On the surface, *Princess Mononoke* is an epic war film, but the most important thing isn't who's fighting, but what's being fought over. It's what surrounds the armies: their environment. Set in an ancient woodland, there's the mystical Spirit of the Forest that has a deer body and human face, the cute but ghostly kodamas who scurry around the trees, and there's the forest itself, which is lush and green and full of magic and mystery. Humans, animals, and magical creatures all have their own plans for the forest. Some want to preserve it, some want to destroy it. But it's clear at the heart of the film is nature, which becomes both the hero and the victim of this story.

Haku and Chihiro

Spirited Away, 2001

When Chihiro enters the magical bathhouse in *Spirited Away*, she encounters men with multiple arms, witches who turn into birds, and cloaked figures with no face who eat everything they see. But it is her meeting with Haku, the River Spirit who has forgotten who he is, that shows the importance of nature to Studio Ghibli. Haku's river has been filled up and is now gone from the human world but Chihiro helps him to remember and she breaks the spell cast on him by the witch Yubaba.

Another moment in the film that shows the importance of nature is Chihiro's contest with the Stink Spirit, a big, brown, sludgy creature with an intense reek. After putting a peg over her nose, Chihiro wrestles with the spirit, eventually pulling trash from its smelly insides. It turns out the Stink Spirit is actually a River Spirit, and humans have filled it with litter, poisoning it; but with Chihiro's helping hand, it is restored to its glorious natural state and it gives her a powerful gift.

Pazu and Sheeta

Laputa: Castle in the Sky, 1986

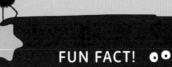

FUN FACT!

A replica of this robot stands on top of the Ghibli Museum in Tokyo (see us standing next to it on page 6).

Laputa: Castle in the Sky is a swashbuckling adventure, but even on the mysterious high-tech flying island of Laputa, there is a meaningful moment of connection with nature. The gigantic robot, who has been wandering alone around the island for countless years, has turned its hand to gardening. And when it meets our young heroes, it gives them a symbol of the peace and harmony of its natural surroundings: a flower.

Pom Poko

Nature has to be protected. If it goes away, we will lose something forever.

In *Pom Poko*, the community of magic Tanuki
creatures are a symbol of the wonder of
our forests and green spaces. Their habitat
is under threat from bulldozers as the city
expands, destroying everything in its path.

My Neighbor Totoro, 1988

How to

DO TOTORO'S DONDOKO DANCE

Have you recently planted a seed and want it to grow really quickly? Well, why not try Totoro's trademark "dondoko" dance? When Satsuki and Mei wake up to see the three Totoro creatures crowding around the patch in their garden where they buried the special seeds, they join in the dance and something magical happens...

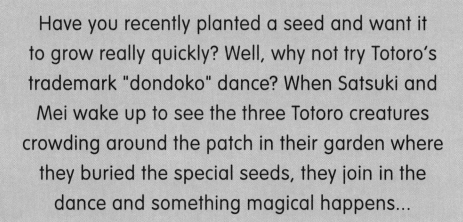

1 Slowly walk around your freshly-seeded patch or plant pot.

2 Now, hop around the patch in formation.

3 Stand in line along one side.

4 Clasp your hands together.

5 Then crouch down and then raise your hands to the sky, reaching up as high as you can.

6 Repeat, with increasing intensity, until—if you're lucky!—sprouts spring and a giant tree grows up into the heavens.

WHO'S WHO AT STUDIO GHIBLI?

. . . .

If you thought the characters on screen were interesting,
just wait until you learn about the real people who made them.

Hayao Miyazaki

JOB:
Director, Writer, Producer

DATE OF BIRTH:
January 5th, 1941

HOMETOWN:
Tokyo

HAYAO MIYAZAKI is an international icon in the world of animation. His films have broken box office records, won prestigious awards, and charmed generations of kids in Japan and around the world. From *Spirited Away* and *Howl's Moving Castle,* to his most recent film, *How Do You Live?*, every Miyazaki movie is a major event.

Not only is he a master of thoughtful storytelling that is full of wisdom regarding the world around us, he is also a versatile and skilled artist and animator. He is able to design his enchanting fantasy worlds, fill them with unique and beguiling characters, and he also plays a hands-on role during the frame-by-frame animation of his films.

Ever since he was a boy, Miyazaki has been obsessed with how things worked, particularly planes and tanks. Even as an adult, he still spends time doodling detailed drawings of these military machines, and submitting them to magazines for people who love to make models.

Spirited Away, 2001

Only Yesterday, 1991

Isao Takahata

JOB:
Director,
Writer, Producer

DATE OF BIRTH:
October 29th, 1935

HOMETOWN:
Ise

ISAO TAKAHATA was a founding director of Studio Ghibli. After meeting a young Hayao Miyazaki, the two formed a strong creative partnership, and worked together on films even before they founded the studio together. He was a slow filmmaker though, and the quick-working Miyazaki described Takahata as being "descended from a giant sloth." Their films are very different, but equally deserving of praise.

Grave of the Fireflies, a story about two kids trying to survive a war, is superb, but also one of the saddest films ever made. *Only Yesterday* is full of the joys of nature and childhood. *Pom Poko* showcases the boundless possibilities of animation, and his final masterpiece, *The Tale of the Princess Kaguya*, is both a fairytale and celebration of art and artists.

Toshio Suzuki

JOB:
Producer and
Former Studio
President

DATE OF BIRTH:
August 19th, 1948

HOMETOWN:
Nagoya

TOSHIO SUZUKI works behind the scenes. He is a man full of stories, and he isn't afraid of stepping into the spotlight and casting himself as the hero behind Studio Ghibli's ongoing success.

Before Ghibli, he was an editor at an anime magazine, Animage, and it was there that he promoted Hayao Miyazaki and Isao Takahata's work, and even published the manga of *Nausicaä of the Valley of the Wind* before it became a blockbuster movie.

At Ghibli, he has had a hand in everything from guiding the concept and production of a film, to overseeing the release and poster designs.

Goro Miyazaki

JOB:
Director, Museum Director

DATE OF BIRTH:
January 21st, 1967

HOMETOWN:
Tokyo

GORO MIYAZAKI never dreamed of following his dad into the world of animation. Instead, he designed parks and public spaces, and he was first brought into the Studio Ghibli family to help design and run the Ghibli Museum.

Toshio Suzuki said that Goro did such a great job on that project, that he thought he'd do just as good a job directing a film. And so, Goro was given the task of making *Tales From Earthsea*. His dad, who had wanted to make an Earthsea film himself, wasn't very pleased.

But Goro is now one of Ghibli's main filmmakers, and has directed *From Up On Poppy Hill* and *Earwig and the Witch*, Ghibli's first film to be made in a computer-generated style rather than drawn by hand.

FUN FACT!

Goro's mom, Akemi Ôta, also had a career in animation. In fact, when Hayao Miyazaki started working at his first animation job, she was senior to him and had already worked on several films!

Joe Hisaishi

JOE HISAISHI's music for *My Neighbor Totoro*, *Princess Mononoke* and *Spirited Away* matches the wildly imaginative animation; his orchestration perfectly captures the wild jazziness of a Catbus, the epic rumbles of war, or the bright, curious melodies of a spirit-filled bathhouse.

All of Hisaishi's musical scores for Miyazaki's films are wonderful, but make sure you listen to his work on *The Tale of the Princess Kaguya*. It's delicate, romantic, and wistful and it was the first, and sadly only time, that he worked with Isao Takahata, and it's one of his very best.

JOB: Composer
DATE OF BIRTH: December 6th, 1950
HOMETOWN: Nakano

The Tale of the Princess Kaguya, 2013

Yoshifumi Kondō

JOB: Animator, Character Designer, Director
DATE OF BIRTH: March 31st, 1950

YOSHIFUMI KONDŌ was one of Ghibli's best. He worked with both Hayao Miyazaki and Isao Takahata on many films, and even directed his own, *Whisper of the Heart*.

Kazuo Oga

JOB: Art Director, Background Artist
DATE OF BIRTH: February 29th, 1952

Behind every great character, there is a breathtaking background, and **KAZUO OGA** painted many of the most memorable landscapes seen across the whole Ghibli film library, from the forests of *My Neighbor Totoro* to the seaside town of *Ponyo*.

Michiyo Yasuda

JOB: Colour Designer
DATE OF BIRTH: April 28th, 1939

If you've ever marvelled at the colours of a Studio Ghibli film, you have **MICHIYO YASUDA** to thank. She started working in animation in the 1960s, and had a hand in many Ghibli projects from *Nausicaä of the Valley of the Wind* to *The Wind Rises*, picking the palette of colors for every film with precision and care.

Spirited Away, 2001

How to

MAKE YOUR OWN FLIPBOOK

Animation is a very time-consuming art form, especially if you're working with Isao Takahata, but if you want to have a try without it taking years and years, you should make a flipbook. Flipbooks illustrate the most basic idea of animation, of still images being transformed to look like they are in motion.

You will need:
- a pen or pencil
- a notebook or block of sticky notes

1

Get a notebook, stack of paper, or block of sticky notes and make sure you're allowed to draw all over them.

2

Turn to the last page and draw a character standing on the bottom edge.

3

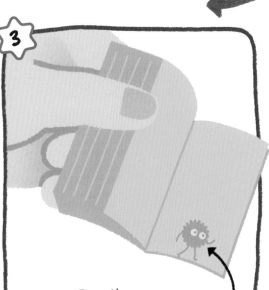

Turn the page over. You will be able to see the first drawing through the page.

4

Use this as a guide and draw the same character again, but change it very slightly. They could start walking, running, or throwing something.

5

Continue this process. Turn the page, draw a bit of movement, and turn the page again.

6

Now hold your flipbook and use your thumb to drag backwards through the pages, revealing each drawing.

Your character has transformed from standing still, to being in motion, that's animation!

Copy this walking cycle to try making a soot sprite walk.

CONTACT   RECOIL   PASSING   HIGH-POINT   CONTACT   RECOIL   PASSING   HIGH-POINT   CONTACT

 Remember, animation can be difficult but the more you practice, the better your animations will become.

GHIBLI'S JAPAN

. . . .

As one of Japan's great cultural ambassadors, Studio Ghibli provides an eye-opening perspective on Japanese history, religion, art, and philosophy, giving many of us our first taste of the country's rich culture. Here is what we can learn about Japan from watching Ghibli films.

In Books

When Studio Ghibli's co-founding director Isao Takahata went to university, he didn't study animation or film, he studied literature; and that passion is a key part of his, and the studio's, work.

Take *The Tale of the Princess Kaguya* for example. It's based on a traditional Japanese story that was written as far back as the early 9th century. That's over one thousand years ago!

The story of the princess who is discovered inside a bamboo plant, is also referenced in *My Neighbors the Yamadas*, which came out 14 years before *The Tale of the Princess Kaguya*.

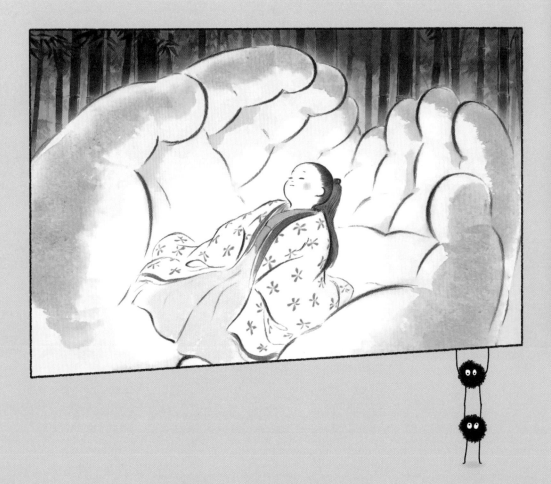

In Art

As well as appreciating literature, being painters and storytellers, Studio Ghibli has a huge appreciation for all of the artists that existed before them and inspired their work.

If you watch Isao Takahata's film *Pom Poko* carefully, in one scene you'll see cameo appearances from Totoro and Kiki, but you'll also see this giant, spooky skeleton. It's not just any set of bones though, it's actually a recreation of a haunting character from *Takiyasha the Witch and the Skeleton Spectre*, a famous image made using woodblocks, created by artist Utagawa Kuniyoshi over 150 years ago.

In Buildings

The bathhouse from *Spirited Away* maybe Ghibli's most memorable location. It was turned into a scale model, shown at an exhibition about architecture in Studio Ghibli's movies. The exhibition was held at the Edo-Tokyo Open-Air Architectural Museum, which restores and maintains historic Japanese buildings, and which actually inspired the design of the bathhouse itself.

It is just a short drive from Ghibli's office, and is a special place for Hayao Miyazaki, the director of *Spirited Away*. He said, "I feel nostalgic here...Especially when I stand here alone in the evening, near closing time and the sun is setting. Tears well up in my eyes."

In Geography

Studio Ghibli's films are filled with magical, wonderful worlds, but they can also be an animated tour guide around the country of Japan, looking at the distinct landscapes and climates that you can find there.

In *Whisper of the Heart*, Shizuku lives in a sleepy suburban town in Western Tokyo. It may seem boring, but Shizuku finds magical moments wherever she goes. The final scene, when Shizuku and Seiji watch the sun rise over the town, shows that there's beauty everywhere if you look for it.

Western Tokyo

Tomonoura

But head out of Tokyo, and the world is your oyster. The breathtaking coastal setting of *Ponyo* is based on the historic port town of Tomonoura, south-west of Tokyo in the Seto Inland Sea region. And the hotel that Jiro and Nahoko visit in *The Wind Rises* is set in the mountainous areas in Nagano, which are known as the Japanese Alps.

Tomonoura

Nagano

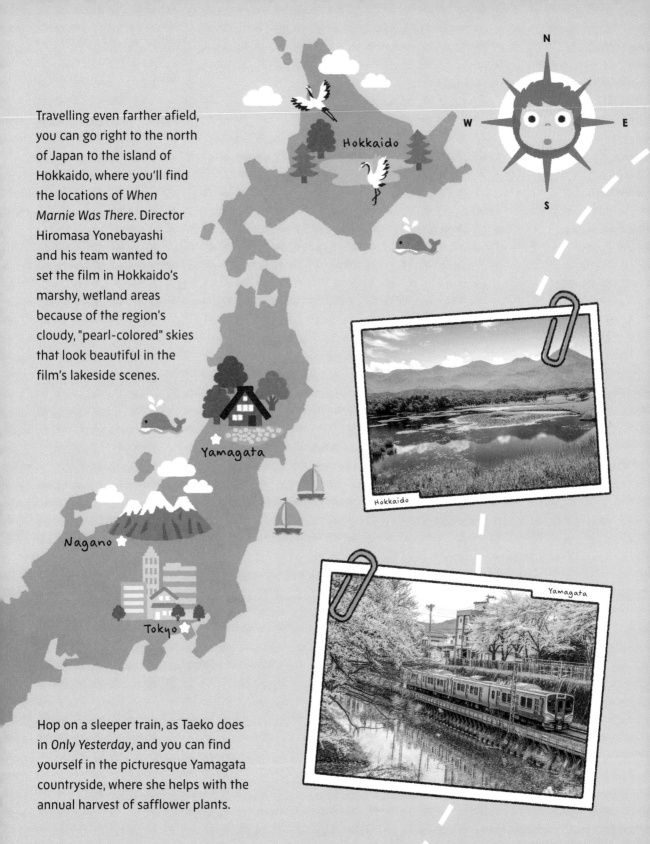

Travelling even farther afield, you can go right to the north of Japan to the island of Hokkaido, where you'll find the locations of *When Marnie Was There*. Director Hiromasa Yonebayashi and his team wanted to set the film in Hokkaido's marshy, wetland areas because of the region's cloudy, "pearl-colored" skies that look beautiful in the film's lakeside scenes.

Hokkaido

Yamagata

Hokkaido

Nagano

Tokyo

Yamagata

Hop on a sleeper train, as Taeko does in *Only Yesterday*, and you can find yourself in the picturesque Yamagata countryside, where she helps with the annual harvest of safflower plants.

In History

It's not always about fantasy worlds and magical creatures in Studio Ghibli films, some of their most beloved and most creative films tell stories set in the real world, rooted in the history of 20th Century Japan.

After World War Two, Japan entered a period of reconstruction and rejuvenation and Goro Miyazaki's film *From Up On Poppy Hill* is a charming recreation of the era, set in 1960s Japan. There are walls with posters of the Tokyo 1964 Olympics on them, construction cranes hanging over the background of some scenes, and exquisitely detailed streets and trams too; for a peek back in time, make sure you give it a watch.

From Up On Poppy Hill, 2011

The Wind Rises is another wartime story, but this one is about a plane designer, inspired by a real man, who loved drawing aircraft; and who would eventually help create a plane that would cause a lot of damage to the world. As well as some stunning dream sequences and a touching romance, there's a re-creation of the hugely destructive Great Kantō earthquake from 1923, the scene is quite intense and really shows how much impact the earthquake had.

The Wind Rises, 2013

Spirits of Japan

The most popular religions in Japan are Shinto and Buddhism, and you will find references to these throughout Ghibli's films.

My Neighbor Totoro, 1988

These statues often appear at moments of danger or magic to guide the hero.

Look out for the Buddhist Rokujizo statues that seem to protect Mei when she is lost in *My Neighbor Totoro,*

...and the Dōsojin Statue that stands at the entrance to the tunnel at the start of Chihiro's adventure in *Spirited Away*.

Hayao Miyazaki believes very strongly in a spirituality that springs from nature. When talking about the forests of *Princess Mononoke*, he said "there is a religious feeling that remains to this day in many Japanese. It is a belief that there is a very pure place deep within our country where people are not to enter. In that place clear water flows and nourishes the deep forests."

Princess Mononoke, 1997

Whisper of the Heart, 1995

How to

SPEAK JAPANESE

Studio Ghibli's films give us a glimpse of the landscape, history, and culture of Japan. They even give us a taste of the Japanese language, too. Maybe one day you might go on a trip to Japan yourself—and if so, here are some handy Japanese phrases that will help you on your way.

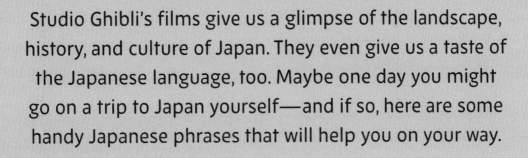

こんにちは

Konnichiwa

ko-n-ni-chi-wa

Hello

私の名前は...

Watashi no namae wa ...

wa-ta-shi-no na-ma-e-wa

My name is...

ありがとう

Arigatoo

a-ri-ga-to-o

Thank you

お名前はなんですか

Onamae wa nandesu ka

o-na-ma-e-wa
na-n-de-su-ka

May I ask your name?

さようなら

Sayoonara

sa-yo-o-na-ra

Goodbye

映画

Eiga

ei-ga

Film

アニメーション

Animeeshon

a-ni-me-e-sho-n

Animation

すすワタリ

Susuwatari

su-su-wa-ta-ri

Soot sprites

スタジオジブリ

Sutajio Jiburi

su-ta-ji-o ji-bu-ri

Studio Ghibli

トトロ

Totoro

To-to-ro

Totoro

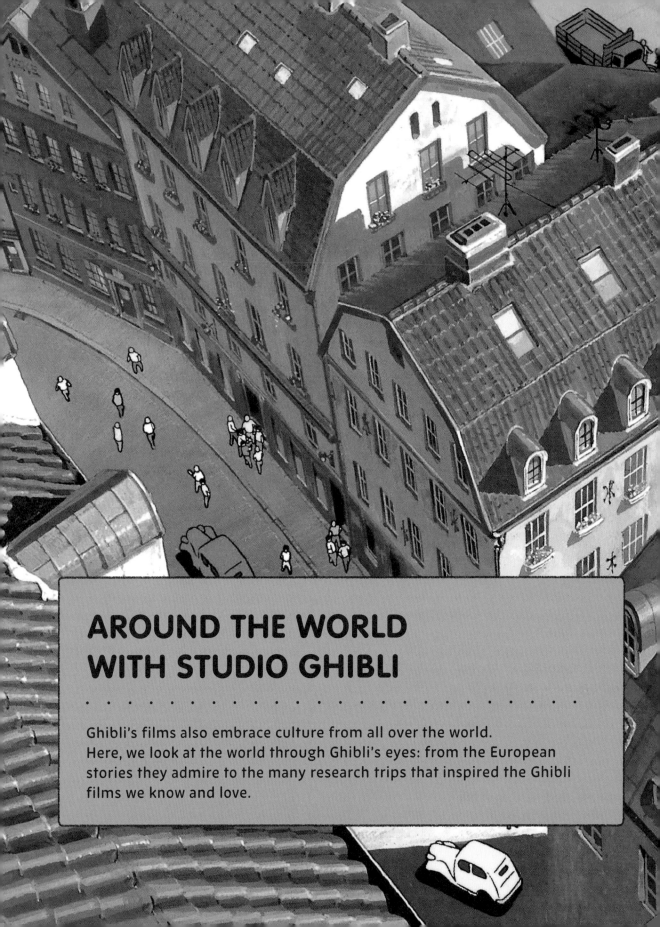

AROUND THE WORLD
WITH STUDIO GHIBLI

· ·

Ghibli's films also embrace culture from all over the world.
Here, we look at the world through Ghibli's eyes: from the European
stories they admire to the many research trips that inspired the Ghibli
films we know and love.

Adaptations From Books

While Studio Ghibli's films have been filled with unique characters and creations, Hayao Miyazaki and his colleagues have always loved stories from around the world. You can see that in the Ghibli projects that have turned English-language books into Japanese films.

For instance, *Howl's Moving Castle* was based on a novel by the beloved British writer Diana Wynne Jones.

Howl's Moving Castle, 2004

Hayao Miyazaki has called American author Ursula K. Le Guin one of his greatest inspirations, and he read her epic *Earthsea* books over and over as he made films ranging from *Nausicaä of the Valley of the Wind* to *Princess Mononoke*. For years, Le Guin had been reluctant to allow anyone to turn her stories into a film, but she gave Ghibli the thumbs up after seeing *My Neighbor Totoro* and becoming a fan of Miyazaki's work. She was less impressed, though, when it was actually his son, Goro Miyazaki, who ended up directing the film, *Tales From Earthsea*!

Tales From Earthsea, 2006

These adaptations show us that the world of Studio Ghibli isn't just confined to Japan, and they are retold in way that could only come from Studio Ghibli. The action may be transferred to Japanese settings, but they give us a new perspective on English language writing—from *Arrietty*, based on Mary Norton's *The Borrowers*, to *When Marnie Was There*, which was adapted from a book by Joan G. Robinson that was a hidden gem in the English-speaking world until Ghibli turned it into a film in 2014.

Arrietty, 2010

Ghibli in Wonderland

Even when their films aren't *direct* adaptations of children's books, Ghibli's films sometimes draw inspiration from European stories.

In *Spirited Away*, Chihiro is whisked away into a surreal world filled with strange and magical creatures, which is very much like Lewis Carroll's *Alice in Wonderland*, a very popular book in Japan. It has been said that the witch sisters, Yubaba and Zeniba, are inspired by characters from that story.

Ghibli's European Tour

Ghibli's films can teach us a lot about Japanese life, about culture, food, religion, and so much more. But not all of Ghibli's films are set in the studio's homeland. On the other side of the world to Ghibli is the continent of Europe, a place that has inspired the studio's filmmakers and which we travel to in a number of their films.

SWEDEN

Soar over Kiki's city of Koriko and you'll see reddish-brown roof tiles, a bustling town square, ancient city walls, and a skyscraping clock tower. After taking a research trip to Europe, the animators were deeply inspired by the buildings and towns in Sweden, so they took what they saw and made it Kiki's home.

Kiki's Delivery Service, 1989

THE MEDITERRANEAN

Farther south in Europe there's a small part of the Mediterranean Sea called the Adriatic, which is in between Italy and Albania, Bosnia and Herzegovina, Croatia, Montenegro, and Slovenia. It's also the home of Porco Rosso. Between flying adventures, Porco relaxes on his secret island, surrounded by beautiful beaches and gleaming ocean waves.

Porco Rosso, 1992

UNITED KINGDOM

Laputa: Castle in the Sky has a unique, old-fashioned look that also feels futuristic too, and that's because of another research trip to Europe. Producer Isao Takahata suggested that director Hayao Miyazaki should visit the UK, which is where a style known as "steampunk" takes a lot of inspiration from.

When he was in the UK, Miyazaki was inspired by the green hills and valleys of Wales, as well as the coal mines that the country relied on, and which the government was closing down. Miyazaki admired the country and the people who fought passionately for their mining communities, and made their home part of his film.

Laputa: Castle in the Sky, 1986

GERMANY

Although it's mostly set in Japan, *The Wind Rises* does take a brief trip to Germany, where plane designer Jiro discovers new kinds of aircraft to help his research. Look at how much detail this plane has, from the ridges on the metal to the rivets that keep it all together, it's no surprise Jiro gets inspired.

The Wind Rises, 2013

From Up on Poppy Hill, 2011

TEST YOUR GHIBLI KNOWLEDGE

You have now traveled the entire world of Studio Ghibli! But how much can you remember from our magical journey through the studio's films? The answers can be found on page 125.

1.
Who is cursed with old age at the start of *Howl's Moving Castle*?

2.
The soot sprites appear in two Studio Ghibli films but can you remember which two?

3.
What type of tree stands next to Mei and Satsuki's house in *My Neighbor Totoro*?

4.
What is Ponyo's favorite food?

5.
Who gives Pazu and Sheeta a flower in *Laputa: Castle in the Sky*?

6.
What is the name of the cat that lives in the Studio Ghibli offices?

7.
How tall is Arrietty?

8.
In *Whisper of the Heart*, what animal does Shizuku follow off the train?

9.
Which country inspired the setting for *Kiki's Delivery Service*?

10.
How many markings does a King Totoro have on his chest?

How Many Have You Seen?

Nausicaä of the Valley of the Wind, 1984

Laputa: Castle in the Sky, 1986

My Neighbour Totoro, 1988

Kiki's Delivery Service, 1989

Only Yesterday, 1991

Porco Rosso, 1992

Pom Poko, 1994

Whisper of the Heart, 1995

Princess Mononoke, 1997

Spirited Away, 2001

The Cat Returns, 2002

Howl's Moving Castle, 2004

Tales From Earthsea, 2006

Ponyo, 2008

Arrietty, 2010

From Up On Poppy Hill, 2011

The Wind Rises, 2013

The Tale of the Princess Kaguya, 2013

When Marnie Was There, 2014

Earwig and the Witch, 2020

Look out for *How Do You Live?*, 2023

1.	Sophie	6.	Ushiko
2.	My Neighbor Totoro and Spirited Away	7.	Four inches
3.	A camphor tree	8.	A cat
4.	Ham!	9.	Sweden
5.	A giant robot	10.	Seven

Index

Alice in Wonderland 115
Andersen, Hans Christian 29
Animage 86
Anna 41, 58
Arrietty 113, 125
Arrietty 16
Ashitaka 12

Baron 27
Borrowers 16
Buddhism 104

Calcifer 55
Carroll, Lewis 115
Catbus 60, 88
cats 26-27
Chihiro 11, 13, 25, 58, 71, 105, 115
cosplay 19-21

Dōsojin statue 105

Earthsea 113,
Earwig and the Witch 87, 125
Edo-Tokyo Open Air
    Architectural Museum 99

Fanning, Dakota and Elle 10
flipbook, make your
    own 90-93
From Up on Poppy Hill 44,
    87, 102, 120, 125

Ghibli food 38-51
Ghibli Museum
    (Tokyo) 6, 7, 73, 87

Ghibliotheque 7
Grave of Fireflies 85

Haku (River Spirit) 11, 71
Hisaishi, Joe 88
How Do You Live? 82, 125
Howl 14
Howl's Moving Castle 14,
    45, 55, 82, 112, 124

Japan 94-105
Japanese phrases 106-109
Jiji 13, 26, 46
Jiro Horikoshi 54, 63, 100, 119
Jones, Diana Wynne 112

Kamajī 31
Kiki 13, 20, 46, 61, 97, 116
Kiki's broom 61
Kiki's Delivery Service 7,
    13, 26, 46, 61, 116, 124
King 27
Kodama 32
kodamas 69
Kondō, Yoshifumi 89
Kuniyoshi, Utagawa 97

Laputa 15, 73
*Laputa: Castle in the
    Sky* 15, 72-73, 118, 124
Le Guin, Ursula K. 113
Lisa 47

Markl 45
Mei 10, 24, 31, 60, 68, 77, 104

Miyazaki, Goro 17, 87, 102, 113
Miyazaki, Hayao 17, 29, 30, 52,
    54, 55, 60, 63, 82-83, 85, 86,
    87, 88, 89, 99, 105, 112, 113, 118
My Neighbor Totoro 7,
    10, 24, 31, 44, 60, 68,
    88, 89, 104, 113, 124
My Neighbors the Yamadas 96

Nahoko 63, 100
National Cat Day 26
nature 66-75, 105
*Nausicaä of the Valley of the
    Wind* 30, 89, 113, 124
*Nausicaä of the Valley of the
    Wind* manga 30, 86
No-Face 25, 43, 58
Norton, Mary 113

Oga, Kazuo 89
Ohmu 30
Only Yesterday 58,
    84, 85, 101, 124
Ôta, Akemi 87

paper glider, how to
    build 62-65
Pazu 15, 21, 72-73
Pom Poko 33, 74-75, 85, 97, 124
Ponyo 17, 28-29, 47, 50, 51, 57
Ponyo 29, 47, 56, 89, 100, 125
Porco Rosso 54, 117
Porco Rosso 54, 117, 124
Princess Mononoke 7, 12,
    32, 69, 88, 105, 113, 124

ramen, how to make
   your own 48-51
River Spirit 71
Robinson, Joan G. 113
robot 6, 73
Rokujizo statues 104

San 12, 13
Satsuki 10, 24, 31, 44, 60, 68, 77
Seiji 100
Setsu 41
Sheeta 72-73
Shinto 104
Shizuku 59, 100
Shō 16
Skeleton Spectre 97
Soot sprites (susuwatari) 31, 93
Sophie 14
Sōsuke 17, 29, 47, 50
Spirit of the Forest 69
Spirited Away 7, 11, 25, 31, 42,
   43, 58, 70-71, 82, 83, 88, 90,
   98-99, 105, 114-115, 123, 124
Stink Spirit 11, 71
Suzuki, Toshio 86, 87
Swamp Bottom 58

Taeko 58, 101
Takahata, Isao 33, 84-85, 86,
   88, 89, 91, 96, 97, 118
Takiyasha the Witch 97
Tales From Earthsea 87, 113, 125
Tanuki 33, 74
The Borrowers 113
The Cat Returns 27, 124

The Little Mermaid 29
The Tale of the Princess
   Kaguya 85, 88, 96, 125
The Wind Rises 54, 63,
   89, 100, 103, 119, 125
Totoro 10, 22, 24, 35,
   60, 68, 77, 97
Dondoko dance, how
   to do it 76-79
how to draw 36-37

Umi 44
Ushiko 27

When Marnie Was There 40,
   41, 57, 58, 101, 113, 125
Whisper of the Heart 59,
   89, 100, 124

Yasuda, Michiyo 89
Yonebayashi, Hiromasa 101
Yubaba 71, 115

Zeniba 58, 115

Published in 2023 by Welbeck Children's Books
An Imprint of Welbeck Children's Limited, part of the Welbeck Publishing Group
Offices in: London - 20 Mortimer Street, London W1T 3JW &
Sydney - Level 17, 207 Kent St, Sydney NSW 2000 Australia
www.welbeckpublishing.com

Design and layout © Welbeck Children's Limited 2023

Text © 2023 Michael Leader and Jake Cunningham

Michael Leader and Jake Cunningham have asserted their moral rights to be identified
as the authors of this Work in accordance with the Copyright Designs and Patents Act 1988.

Editor: Gemma Farr
Designer: Sam James
Layout Design: Emily Calnan
Illustrator: Lucy Zhang
Consultant: Dr Seiko Harumi of the School of Oriental and African Studies (SOAS)

ISBN: 978 1 80338 124 4
Printed in Heshan, China
10 9 8 7 6 5 4 3 2 1

Disclaimer: Any names, characters, trademarks, service marks and trade names detailed in this
book is the property of their respective owners and is used solely for identification and reference
purposes. This book is a publication of Welbeck Children's Books, part of Welbeck Publishing Group
and has not been licensed, approved, sponsored or endorsed by any person or entity.

The publishers would like to thank the following sources for their kind permission to reproduce the pictures in this book.

4 Everett Collection Inc/Alamy Stock Photo; 6 Private Collection; 8-9 Photo 12/Alamy Stock Photo; 10 1988 Studio Ghibli; 11 United Archives GmbH/Alamy Stock Photo; 12 Photo 12/Alamy Stock Photo; 13 Photo 12/Alamy Stock Photo; 14 United Archives GmbH/Alamy Stock Photo; 15 Photo 12/Alamy Stock Photo; 16 2010 Studio Ghibli – NDHDMTW; 17 Moviestore Collection Ltd/Alamy Stock Photo; 18 Album/Alamy Stock Photo; 22-23 Everett Collection Inc/Alamy Stock Photo; 24 Photo 12/Alamy Stock Photo; 25 2001 Studio Ghibli – NDDTM; 26 Everett Collection Inc/Alamy Stock Photo; 27 AJ Pics/Alamy Stock Photo; 28 (top) Photo 12/Alamy Stock Photo; 28 (centre) Maximum Film/Alamy Stock Photo; 28 (bottom) Cinematic Collection/Alamy Stock Photo; 30 1984 Studio Ghibli – H; 31 Photo 12/Alamy Stock Photo; 32 Photo 12/Alamy Stock Photo; 33 Photo 12/Alamy Stock Photo; 34 1988 Studio Ghibli; 38-39 2001 Studio Ghibli – NDDTM; 40 2014 Studio Ghibli – NDHDMTK; 41 2014 Studio Ghibli – NDHDMTK; 42-43 2001 Studio Ghibli – NDDTM; 44 2011 Chizuru Takahashi - Tetsuro Sayama - Studio Ghibli – NDHDMT; 45 2004 Studio Ghibli – NDDMT; 46 1988 Studio Ghibli; 47 2008 Studio Ghibli – NDHDMT; 48 2008 Studio Ghibli – NDHDMT; 52-53 Everett Collection Inc/Alamy Stock Photo; 54 1992 Studio Ghibli – NN; 55 2004 Studio Ghibli – NDDMT; 56 Cinematic Collection/Alamy Stock Photo; 57 Moviestore Collection Ltd/Alamy Stock Photo; 58 2001 Studio Ghibli – NDDTM; 59 1995 Aoi Hiiragi/Shueisha - Photo – NH; 60 1988 Studio Ghibli; 61 Photo 12/Alamy Stock Photo; 62 2013 Studio Ghibli – NDHDMTK; 66-67 Everett Collection Inc/Alamy Stock Photo; 68 Album/Alamy Stock Photo; 69 1997 Studio Ghibli – ND; 70-71 Album/Alamy Stock Photo; 72-73 AJ Pics/Alamy Stock Photo; 74-75 Photo 12/Alamy Stock Photo; 76 Everett Collection Inc/Alamy Stock Photo; 80-81 Moviestore Collection Ltd/ Alamy Stock Photo; 82 Newscom/Alamy Stock Photo; 83 Maximum Film/Alamy Stock Photo; 84 Maximum Film/Alamy Stock Photo; 85 Sipa US/Alamy Stock Photo; 86 Dominique Charriau/Getty Images; 87 Franco Origlia/Getty Images; 88 (top) Simone Ferraro/Alamy Stock Photo; 88 (bottom) Photo 12/Alamy Stock Photo; 90 2001 Studio Ghibli – NDDTM; 94-95 Photo 12/Alamy Stock Photo; 96 2013 Hatake Jimusho - Studio Ghibli – NDHDMTK; 97 1994 Hatake Jimusho - Studio Ghibli – NH; 98 Photo 12/Alamy Stock Photo; 100 (top right) anju901/Shutterstock; 100 (left) hayakato/Shutterstock; 100 (bottom left) amnat11/Shutterstock; 101 (top) rayints/Shutterstock; 101 (bottom) weniiliou/Shutterstock; 102 2011 Chizuru Takahashi - Tetsuro Sayama - Studio Ghibli – NDHDMT; 103 Photo 12/Alamy Stock Photo; 104 1988 Studio Ghibli; 105 (top) 2001 Studio Ghibli – NDDTM; 105 (bottom) 1997 Studio Ghibli – ND; 106 1995 Aoi Hiiragi/Shueisha - Studio Ghibli – NH; 108 Entertainment Pictures/Alamy Stock Photo; 109 Album/Alamy Stock Photo; 110-111 Photo 12/Alamy Stock Photo; 112 Album/Alamy Stock Photo; 113 (top) Photo 12/Alamy Stock Photo; 113 (bottom) Cinematic Collection/Alamy Stock Photo; 114-115 2001 Studio Ghibli – NDDTM; 116 1988 Studio Ghibli; 117 1992 Studio Ghibli – NN; 118 1986 Studio Ghibli; 119 2013 Studio Ghibli – NDHDMTK; 120 Everett Collection Inc/Alamy Stock Photo; 123 Photo 12/Alamy Stock Photo

Every effort has been made to acknowledge correctly and contact the source and/or copyright
holder of each picture and Welbeck Publishing Group apologises for any unintentional
errors or omissions, which will be corrected in future editions of this book.